D1348001

Too Late to Learn to Drive

Dementia, visual perception
and the meaning of pictures.

Helen J Bate
B.A.Dip.Arch.B.A.(Hons)M.A.

I2614862

I have been involved in different types of visual communication for 40 years. Originally an Architect, I retrained as an illustrator and in 2005 I began a second career in publishing, working in both children's illustration and books for people with dementia.

It was when my mother developed dementia in the 1990's that I became aware of the many unforseen problems this terrible illness could cause in the later stages. Witnessing the difficulties my Mum had experienced, I wanted to try and make a small difference to people like her who, because of dementia could no longer enjoy their favourite books and magazines.

This eventually resulted in the establishment of 'Pictures to Share' as a social enterprise and the creation of a range of illustrated books that help to improve the quality of life for many thousands of people with dementia across the UK and overseas.

Our work shows repeatedly how people with later stage dementia can benefit from the right type of pictures and books. Designers and carers working in the field of dementia care need to understand how later stage dementia can affect visual perception of two dimensional imagery. If they do, they are better prepared to provide resources and activities that really make a difference.

This book attempts to explain some of the theories and principles behind the success of our books. It does not aim to be an academic publication. If the academic world wants to further explore or challenge anything in these pages, at least the conversation has begun.

Helen Bate
October 2014

Contents

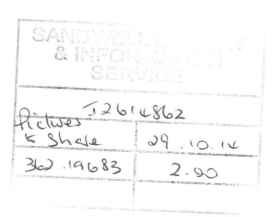

SANDWELL LIBRARY
& INFORMATION
SERVICE

Pictures   I2614862
to share   29.10.14
362.19683   2.90

My parents Jenny and Doug enjoying a day in the country in the 1960's

Introduction

"Is it too late in the day for me to learn to drive, Doug?"

This was the question that my mother Jenny asked one night when talking in her sleep. It was remarkable because she had severe dementia and could no longer speak in sentences in her waking hours. However, it was also thought provoking because she'd never expressed an interest in learning to drive before. My father Doug was always the driver in the family and was now her full-time carer. He had been rushed into hospital that day, and with him had gone her safety, security and independence. Maybe in her mind, the ability to drive a car symbolized having control over her life at a time when she had none.

Nobody would expect that someone with advanced dementia could learn to drive. Driving is an activity that requires sophisticated, complex and extraordinary abilities in visual processing. As drivers we have to see and understand the road layout in front, behind and to the side of us. In the space of seconds, we interpret complex road signs and traffic signals and identify and make decisions about unexpected hazards and the intentions of other road users. Our brain has to process all this visual information immediately and then tell us what action to take to enable us and other road users to remain safe.

We may all understand that the visual processing abilities that safe driving demands are badly affected by dementia; but we rarely consider how these problems also prevent people interacting with the large variety of visual media that is such a hugely important part of our modern world.

We assume that when people with dementia stop reading books, their favourite newspaper or magazine, and when they're no longer engaged by pictures hanging on the wall, family photographs or programmes on the television, that they have reached a stage of dementia that means they are just not capable of enjoying this type of activity any more. But this is usually not the case. It just means that we as carers are not providing the right material; we are not adapting our care to the person's needs.

In his book 'Dementia Care - *the Adaptive Response*', Paul Smith explains the 'adaptive approach' to dementia care and why it is so important.

"Dementia can consist of a regular series of 24-hour catastrophic, acutely challenging and stressful experiences. Relief and respite from 'challenge' becomes elusive if the environment and the 'care' promoted do not adapt and evolve to their changing needs. Eventually the person is overwhelmed and retreats from life."

We can never give those with advanced dementia back the sense of freedom and independence that driving may have given them unless we supply a friendly full-time personal chauffeur. But we can give them back the opportunity to enjoy pictures and the printed word if we adapt books and provide them in the right format.

Ours is a society that for the last 50 years has depended heavily on the visual image and the written word for its entertainment. A suitable illustrated book can allow someone with advanced dementia to enjoy and share their feelings about art, poetry, history, stories, humour, song, and sadness. Providing them with such a book can be like handing them and their families a lifeline to a lost part of themselves. It can help to reconnect them with the world in a small but important way.

The following chapters explore why pictures are so important in our society. In them we look at the reasons why people with dementia can have difficulty understanding images and what what can be done to mitigate these problems. We examine what types of image and presentation can be effective, why some images can be more successful than others in promoting meaningful engagement and why some types of images should never be used.

Chapter 1
The meaning of pictures

"We are intensely visual creatures, and we live in a world that is largely orientated to sight."

Eric R Kandel

Being able to see the world around us is, for sighted people, the most important ability they have. 50% of all the information coming into our brain arrives through our eyes. Since the earliest civilisations, pictures, or two-dimensional images have played an important role within almost every society, and in modern times their impact and influence on our lives is immense.

When we develop severe dementia and our ability to get out and about in the real world is limited, pictures can play an important role in making us feel that we are still engaging with life.

But not all types of pictures are helpful. Some pictures can lead to disengagement and withdrawal, some to anxiety or distress.

If we are to use pictures successfully with people in the later stages of dementia, we need to understand three things;

1. The reason pictures engage us as human beings

2. How our brains makes sense of pictures

3. What difference it makes when we have dementia

Family photographs like the wedding group from 1910 (top) began as rather formal images of memorable events. By the 1960's family photographs became a way for everyone to capture small moments of everyday life. These can be far more interesting, especially for those with later stage dementia. They may be unable to recognize anyone shown in the photographs, but they may recognize and relate to the activity shown in the later family 'snap'.

Pictures from our past

Family photographs first became widely available at the end of the 19th century. By the mid 20th century most families took their own photographs. These were often more interesting than the earlier studio portraits but with cheap cameras and poor camera skills, the images were often grainy, out of focus and badly composed.

Family photographs are commonly used when people develop dementia. Relatives and carers will often use them to help someone remember past events or people that were important to them. 'Life story work' uses these personal photographs and in the earlier stages of dementia they can help people retain a better sense of their own identity, as well as helping others to see the whole person rather than the diagnosis.

However the perceptual problems of mid to later stages of dementia can create difficulties with the recognition and interpretation of many family photographs. When presented with an image of people that they no longer recognize people may 'switch off' or may feel frustrated and that they have failed in some way. Even a wedding photo can become just another irrelevant image for someone who doesn't remember getting married. The following is typical of the experience of many family carers.

"In the last two years my Dad has forgotten everything really. My Mum died in 1995 and he missed her terribly, but now he doesn't even know he was ever married. He doesn't know who I am, but he knows I'm somebody very important and he enjoys us going to visit him. His wedding photograph is in his bedroom but often we'll find it put away in a drawer."

Some believe that the emphasis on life story work can even be detrimental for people with severe dementia. Whilst it's essential for fully understanding the individual, in focussing primarily on the historical self we may fail to recognise the importance of the here and now. When the person with dementia has forgotten the past or can no longer talk about it, carers may feel the opportunity for any meaningful engagement has passed and they may have little idea what they can do to find new subjects for communication.

RUMPELSTILTSKIN

When we no longer recognize close relatives, our favourite childhood picture books may still tap directly into our most personal emotional memories.

Good quality pictures showing familiar activities can provide meaningful reminiscence even when we can no longer talk about our past.

Personal reminiscence
in the later stages

Many care homes use old street scenes or photographs of local landmarks on their walls, with the intention that their residents will have strong associations with this type of image and will be able to enjoy them. This type of picture can be very effective in creating a talking point between those with earlier stage dementia and care staff and may prompt memories about certain life events or the history of the community. As long as memories remain intact and as long as someone can verbalize them, then this type of image can have great value.

However, views of local streets or landmarks will be far less meaningful to the growing number of people who may have moved from elsewhere to be nearer family members, or those who spent their formative years and early lives in other places, or even in other cultures. This type of image will also be less meaningful to those in the later stages of dementia who may find the complexity of the images too challenging, or who can no longer remember or verbalize their stories. In the later stages people need to have a much stronger and more personal emotional connection with an image.

Some images that aren't family photographs or local street scenes can be part of the fabric of our lives and identity in a very personal way. If you spent your working life making cheese, or you had a special childhood picture book, a poster of your teenage heart-throb (in my case Paul Newman) or a favourite music album cover then it's likely that these will always be images that have very special and very personal meaning. That very personal meaning won't be shared by the general population but may if we are lucky, be understood by family or friends. For people with dementia these type of images can be an excellent next step to follow life story work.

The difficulty lies in knowing what images might have meaning for someone and locating the right quality of image to use.

If we all took the time to make a high quality scrapbook of all the various images that have held real meaning for us throughout our lives, it would provide a wonderful resource for our family to use with us if we develop dementia.

Bad news stories

Since the early days of photography, many global events have been recorded in photographs and film. News photography has made events that we have never experienced very real to us, and we have grown accustomed to seeing disasters in far distant places unfold before our eyes.

Soldiers 'going over the top' in Flanders, the collapsing twin towers of New York, images of children starving in Africa or the wild and destructive force of a Japanese tsunami. A tiny percentage of us really witnessed any of these terrible things but through the visual imagery used, we all feel we have a personal connection to these events and many more. Bad news events have become part of our life experience in a way that they never could without photography.

The cultural historian Maurice Berger, argues that news photographs are traumatic because the viewer is powerless to prevent the distressing or frightening events shown in the photograph. Someone looking at a picture also experiences it primarily at an emotional level. In a healthy adult the emotional impact of even a very unpleasant event or picture can be reduced and neutralized by evaluating and reappraising the experience in unemotional terms (Kandel 2012) They have effective control mechanisms within their brain which can allow them to 'get over it.' People with dementia are unable to do this and they may be left feeling distressed, frightened and anxious for some time, even when the picture is long forgotten.

When we have dementia, an inability to always differentiate between a picture and reality and our inability to effectively reappraise our own negative emotions about the image, can lead to some seemingly innocent pictures creating distress.

This painting opposite shows two small children paddling at the seaside, a popular subject used with many people with dementia for reminiscence. However this image can create real anxiety in some people with dementia.

Children in the Sea, 1909, Sorolla y Bastida, Joaquin (1863-1923)
Museo Sorolla, Madrid, Spain, Bridgeman Images

The girls are apparently alone and the swirling of the water appears to be quite powerful and slightly menacing. The posture of the girls seems tense and they appear to be focussing on the water swirling around them. This in turn will focus the viewers attention on the water and those with dementia, especially those who are parents, may well be fearful that the children are in real danger. Unable to rationalize that this is just a painting, they may feel powerless to protect the vulnerable children from the disaster that may be about to unfold.

If a caring parent or adult was shown with the children, or the water was clearly very shallow, or the children could be seen smiling reassuringly at the viewer, the emotional response would be far more positive and the picture would be unlikely to cause distress.

Pictures that give us information

Informative images are used in many ways from textbooks of engineering drawings and interpretation boards at places we visit, to television, book and magazine images of people, holiday destinations, wildlife, history and hobbies.

Thousands of images help us by providing information to make our daily life easier. A map of the underground, a computer image of what our new kitchen will look like, road maps we use to get from A to B and diagrams that help us put together flat pack furniture. We teach our children and ourselves about the world by the use of images and diagrams, television documentaries and cookery programmes.

There is a growing industry dedicated to special signage that aims to make life easier for people with dementia. Using simplified images they aim to help people to find their way around. Care homes may use images of food to explain the menu for people with dementia. All these images can be important in helping people make sense of their environment and so can help to improve their quality of life.

But other types of informative images can have a deeper personal significance that may still have meaning when someone has severe dementia, and we should not ignore this possibility for making connections with them.

A man who worked as a mechanic may enjoy a technical illustration of an engine; a keen hill walker may enjoy looking at ordnance survey maps; people may be able to recognize a map of their home town and someone who drove trains for a living may enjoy a map of the rail or tube networks where they spent their working life. An Architect who spent their life drawing buildings may still enjoy looking at architectural drawings and a keen amateur dressmaker may well still enjoy fashion illustrations.

Success in engaging those with dementia using these type of images will very much depend on the amount of earlier exposure to such images and how much familiarity and understanding of them is retained.

If life-long exposure to certain types of specialist image means it is still relatively easy for someone to understand them when they have dementia, then the images can potentially remain a source of comfort, and a link with their past lives.

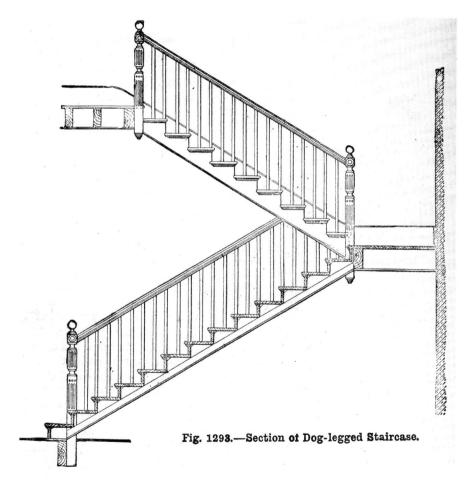

Fig. 1293.—Section of Dog-legged Staircase.

Familiarity with technical drawings may mean that this type of image may still be enjoyed by someone with dementia who worked in the building industry.

Cultural reminiscence & advertising

In every culture there are shared images that are recognised by most of the population. Images of royalty, film stars, sportsmen and women or politicians; familiar objects might include a telephone box, 'Big Ben', a flat iron or a thatched country cottage, iconic advertising images or famous packaging designs.

We may well recognize these type of images when we have dementia and they frequently crop up in reminiscence sessions. However the relevance of these events and people is primarily cultural and not personal. We may know who Winston Churchill is and what he achieved, but it will probably have little direct relevance to our emotional memories that are the main focus of importance to us in later stage dementia. We may be able to recognize a photograph of Marilyn Monroe, but how much more is there to say or feel about it unless she was our own choice of adolescent

'pinup'? We may recognize a photograph of a fish, but unless we were a fisherman or a fishmonger, that picture will have little relevance to us personally.

Recognition is not the same as relevance, and relevance is what is important to us when we have dementia.

Many British people would recognize this as an AA box, but unless they built them or they used to be an AA patrolman it will probably have very little emotional significance or interest for them if they have later stage dementia.

The advertising industry has long understood the power of the visual image. As a result we are bombarded by advertising images in magazines, newspapers, on posters at the bus stop or in the railway station, on television and on the internet. The general population usually underestimate the impact this advertising has on them and their emotions.

But most people with dementia are no longer susceptible to the ploys of the advertising industry. They are no longer concerned with living a certain lifestyle, watching the latest blockbuster, having the latest technology or following the latest fashion. But in many care homes, old adverts never die and they crop up again and again either as decoration on the walls or in the form of 'reminiscence therapy'. But what are we reminding people of? Does it have value just because people recognize it or does it again need to have a more specific relevance to have any real meaning? The poster below advertises a 1960's Stevie Wonder concert that I attended as a 13 year old. It means little to my current family or friends but it reminds me and the friends I went with of what it felt like to be those excited teenage girls. It taps into our emotional memories.

It is not enough for a person with dementia to recognize an advert or packaging from the past. To have real meaning for them it has to have a very particular relevance specific to the emotional memories of the individual. To have any significant meaning to others, an image has to have an aesthetic value that over-rides its role as a reminiscence aid. If the aesthetic value of an advertising image is strong enough then we are really getting into the realm of 'art', and that is something altogether different.

So what is 'Art'?

and why some pictures have the power to talk to us

Museums and art galleries display many varieties of visual art from ancient frescos to modern video installations. These images are not always conventionally beautiful and might even be visually repulsive. So what's the purpose of art?

Many would say the purpose of art is to communicate with us and make us think about ourselves and our world. Others would say art in some way feeds our spirit and provides meaning to our existence. When people have dementia it doesn't mean they're unable to appreciate art. But it does mean they need art that can communicate effectively with them without being too challenging.

All pictures initially emotionally engage the viewer at a subconscious level. This engagement may draw the viewer toward the image or make them turn away. How often have you walked past a picture in a hospital corridor or on an advertising hoarding and not paid any attention to it? Attracting someone with dementia to pay more attention to a picture will depend on the size and clarity of the image, but also its artistic quality. It therefore matters who has produced that image. It is the visual literacy and creativity of an 'artist' that allows them to produce an image that has a real power to reach other people in a meaningful way.

The images that really talk to people are produced with a skill and an understanding of the visual image as a method of unspoken communication.

The viewer may feel that they are simply responding to 'something they like' not realizing that they are in fact responding to the skill of the artist and the aesthetic quality of the image. So when a dementia care home or hospital is looking for 'art' for its walls how do they decide what to choose? Are the pictures they choose contributing in a meaningful way to the wellbeing of their residents or patients with severe dementia? Does it matter whether they have real artistic quality or whether they are 'kitsch' and have been created by someone with little understanding of art as meaningful communication?

Illustration opposite - Butterflies' by Ann Bridges www.ann-bridges.com

In his book 'The Tell-Tale Brain', Vilayanur S. Ramachandran explains how aesthetic quality "involves the proper and effective deployment of certain artistic universals, whereas kitsch merely goes through the motions, as if to make a mockery of the principles without a genuine understanding of them."

The artistic universals identified and defined by Ramachandran include ideas about grouping of elements, exaggeration or simplification of elements, contrast, semi-concealment, avoidance of the most obvious logical solution, the use of regularity and symmetry, and the use of metaphor. He suggests that one reason for the appeal of true art may be that it "conveys nuances of meaning and subtleties of mood that can only be dimly apprehended or conveyed through spoken language".

So what relevance does the aesthetic quality of pictures have when we are talking about images for people with more severe dementia who are finding it difficult to making meaningful connections with the world and the people around them?

If 'art' can talk directly to the emotions and inner being without the need for verbal reasoning and explanation, then people with dementia who have difficulty communicating have potentially much more than most of us to gain from exposure to it.

People with later stage dementia are not able to analyse complex conceptual art. Their cognitive disabilities mean that they cannot work hard at understanding a two dimensional image. The image must speak directly to them without the need for too many sophisticated thought processes.

So how do you find pictures that can be understood and enjoyed by people with dementia? What is it about an image that means it will be more likely to engage someone with severe cognitive problems? The answers lie in understanding how our brains understand the visual image and what can go wrong with these processes.

Chapter 2
Understanding what we see

Few people appreciate the complex neurological processes that their brain undertakes every time they look at a picture, and so they can have little understanding of how this might be compromised in those with dementia.

When we see an image, information from our eyes is immediately sent to the amygdala, the emotional centre of the brain. Even before we are aware of what we are looking at, we are responding to this information and deciding how to react. Is what we are looking at something that we should avoid or engage with?

Once the amygdala has registered what our eyes can see, our brain then decides whether to pay any attention to it. Capturing attention is the first challenge when selecting images for people with dementia. If a picture does not immediately engage us, then we have probably fallen at the first hurdle. Successfully capturing attention is dependent on the immediate impact of seeing an image and the unconscious processes that our mind goes through.

"Attention is driven by a variety of cognitive factors, including intention, interest, previous knowledge recalled through memory, context, unconscious motivation, and instinctual urges." (Kandel 2012)

Engaging us - Seeing lines

A line on a page is the simplest form of visual communication. A line drawing of a face is instantly understood by almost everyone across the world. It is a mystery how the outline drawing is so instantly recognized when there is no such thing as an outline in the natural world. But the ease with which we recognize line drawings tells us something of how our visual system works.

Even when we are looking at the real world around us, our brain constructs simple lines around the edges of objects we can see to differentiate them from their background. All the time that our eyes are open, orientation cells in the primary visual cortex are creating these line drawings of the scene before us. When looking at a two-dimensional image we also use this innate ability to understand what we're seeing through the creation of lines. We identify separate objects in a picture by mentally instead of unconsciously drawing lines around them and deciding initially whether we should be looking at the object or the background.

When looking at this colour photograph, we first subconsciously draw outlines around the key elements and identify which are the objects and which is the background.

Our brain will then process more of the information by identifying and recognizing the shapes, tones, shadows and patterns within the image; the foam of the waves, the posture of the people, the nature of the lighting and the style of the clothes.

A monochrome image may be preferred by someone with dementia. This is probably because the full colour version of the photograph, by giving us maximum visual information, is even more complex for our brains to process and interpret.

However, some people with dementia respond very well to colour images so we should not automatically assume that because they have dementia, they will prefer black and white photographs.

This type of identification processing seems to be affected in people with dementia causing problems in object recognition within two-dimensional images, and in understanding some three-dimensional scenes. People may not be able to clearly differentiate what they are looking at because two or three shapes or colours are merging together and the outline becomes confused.

Why is this image confusing?

When we try and draw outlines around the sheep in this photograph, many lines seem to merge together and identifying the sheep becomes more of a challenge. The fact that they are lying down so we cannot see their full outline, will also mean they are more difficult for someone with dementia to identify.

Some people with dementia will recognize the horns or the faces and identify them as either sheep or goats, but the image may distress them because they can't make complete sense of what they are seeing.

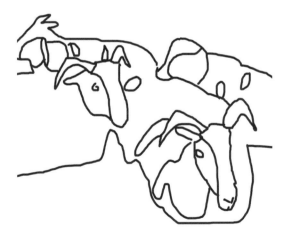

Engaging us -
Seeing what isn't there

If objects are partially hidden, a healthy person will make subconscious judgements about what the partially hidden objects are by 'filling in the gaps'. In a healthy brain neurons in the visual cortex subconsciously complete the outline of a partially hidden object so making sense of the image.

"neurons in the primary visual cortex V2 and V3, respond to a virtual line as effectively as to a real line. As a result, these neurons are capable of completing contours, an ability that accounts for the phenomenon Gestaltists call closure."
(Kandel 2012)

Our brain does not have to work too hard to fill in the missing parts of the image to the right and this may also be achievable for most people with dementia.

But when someone has advanced dementia, they can often no longer make the neurological connections necessary to 'fill in the gaps' and so cannot understand the image. A picture may become a puzzle that cannot be solved and this can be distressing. We can understand this better if we try to make sense of the image to the right. We just cannot tell what it might be. There are not enough clues.

When we can see the whole object it's clear what it is.

People with later stage dementia need many more visual clues than a healthy person. They often cannot visualise the parts of the image that are missing and without the missing parts, an image can become impossible to decipher.

So people with dementia can more easily understand images if the shape and context of an object is clear, and objects are shown in their entirety.

Seeing depth and three dimensions

Depth perception allows us to understand that a picture on a two dimensional 'canvas' is depicting a three-dimensional scene. We are looking at a flat page but we understand that we are looking at a scene of fields with mountains in the distance, or a street with cars that are close to us or far away.

In order to understand that we are looking at a three dimensional image we have to differentiate the objects in the image from their background. As we have seen, this is easier if we can mentally draw outline around the objects. In complex images such as the one below, we also have to decide which are the important objects we should focus on, and which objects are just part of the general background providing overall context.

The ability to understand that a picture can depict a three-dimensional scene depends upon visual processing skills learned in infancy.

We know that the relative size of objects within a picture means that a man in the distance is smaller than a man in the foreground. This knowledge may be disrupted in dementia and someone may believe that a small man and a large man are very different in size and not just a long way apart.

We understand occlusion; that an object partly hidden by another object will be behind it. This understanding may also be disrupted by dementia and the person may see the two objects as one object that makes no sense.

We understand the idea of linear perspective; that railway lines will get closer together the further away they are. We see warmer colours as closer to us than cooler colours. We know that there will be a shadow thrown on one side of an object and this shadow is usually thrown by an overhead light such as the sun. It is hard to tell if the understanding of these principles is affected by dementia.

Colour itself is also constructed by the brain and many people will see colours differently. The problems that people with dementia face in seeing colour undoubtedly varies from individual to individual. Some people with dementia appear to prefer black and white images, whilst some like colour images. As a rule brighter colours and stronger contrasts within an image appear to make images easier for those with dementia to engage with and enjoy. The emotional impact of different colours may be another reason why some people with dementia like some colourful images. The positive effects of warm, cheerful and soothing colours can be achieved through art as well as in interior decor..

Identifying what we see

When we look around us in our everyday life, we have many clues to identify the objects we see. The setting may be a street, our kitchen or a farmyard. The actual size of an object will give us more clues, from a large building to a tiny mosquito. Things may have a sound or a smell associated with them and if in doubt what something is, we may walk around an object to see it from a different viewpoint.

Pictures are far more complex to understand. They are just marks on a flat piece of paper and we bring in a highly sophisticated level of processing to identify what these marks are supposed to represent.

As we've seen, we differentiate an object by drawing outlines, and separating it from the background. But once we have identified something as an object, we need to then identify what the object is.

We do this by categorizing it — initially as maybe a building, an animal, a plant, a person, a machine or a piece of furniture. We then further categorize it by identifying it as something within that wider group; a school building, a giraffe, a cabbage, a policeman, a lawn mower or a wardrobe. In the final stage we determine what relationship the object has to us; its our school, the giraffe we saw at the zoo, the type of cabbage we buy at the supermarket, the policeman interviewed on the TV, our lawn mower or the wardrobe we're thinking of buying for our child's bedroom.

This collection of images illustrates the huge diversity in the type of images we might be faced with every day. Images may be photographs, paintings or drawings. The subjects within images may be real trees, buildings, people or animals. They may be artistic representations of trees, buildings, people or animals. They may even be images of objects that are themselves artistic representations of trees, buildings, people or animals.

With two-dimensional images we also categorize according to the media. It may be a moving image on a screen, a still photograph, a pencil drawing, a painting, an old fashioned print, a stylized or an abstract representation of something.

In this photograph of a baby at a mirror, it is easy to recognize a child, but it would be difficult for many people with dementia to understand that it is not two babies. The correct interpretation of this photograph depends on complex neurological processes that may be too difficult for someone who has significant problems with visual processing.

It is no wonder that there is so much opportunity for the process of identifying imagery to fail when someone has dementia. We can help to remove much of the difficulty from the process by using images that are easier to interpret, but there will still be times when people incorrectly identify people or objects or cannot decipher what an image is about. This is not usually a problem if we are not asking them to identify images with a certain purpose (as often is the case in reminiscence work). But we may sometimes believe that people are mistaken when they aren't.

One lady taking part in a reminiscence session using Pictures to Share books in the care home where she lives was adamant that in the photograph of two ladies delivering milk (opposite), the lady in the glasses was her aunt. The staff were amazed to discover when she produced family photos to compare them, that sure enough it was.

On the milk round/Reg Speller/Hulton Archive/Getty Images

This particular photograph is also a good example of images showing people looking directly out of the page. These are images that often have the power to successfully capture attention and engage people with dementia.

Seeing faces, people and emotions

Many people with severe dementia will respond well to a human face whether it is a real person in front of them or a powerful two-dimensional image. This is a natural part of being human. As a baby, the human face is the first thing that we learn to process visually. But when we see a face, our brain carries out a complex neurological process.

The brain has six discrete regions specialized for face recognition that connect directly to the prefrontal cortex, the area concerned with evaluation of beauty, moral judgement, and decision-making, and to the amygdala, the regions of the brain that orchestrate emotion.

Recognition of a face is therefore a more complex process and one that someone with dementia may struggle with. But often it is not the recognition of a face in an image that is important, but the direction of the gaze and the emotions that the face is expressing. This will affect how someone with dementia responds to that image.

Pictures that contain a human face looking directly out of the page appear to engage someone with dementia more successfully than a picture of a face looking away from the viewer. Portrait painters have long understood the power of the direct gaze and it is a power that can help people with dementia to engage with an image.

"We have a stronger reaction to direct eye contact, because only direct visual contact activates effectively the dopaminergic system of the brain, which is associated with anticipation of reward and therefore with approach"
(Kandel 2012)

Another important aspect of the human face in a two-dimensional image for people with dementia is the message that the face and its expression is giving the viewer. A distressed or angry face may evoke negative responses that make the person with dementia feel upset long after the memory of the image has gone. This type of image should therefore not be used.

A happy or thoughtful face will often make the viewer feel happy or thoughtful. A cheeky laughing face may make the viewer feel like laughing.

A picture of someone feeling melancholy can help those with dementia to talk about feelings of sadness that they may be experiencing. This is not a bad thing if it is giving the person an opportunity to express their feelings to a receptive listener who responds in a caring manner.

The appearance of a face with a particular hairstyle, hat or jewellery, together with the expression of the face - whether sad, happy, surprised or angry, and the context of the face - what is happening in the image… all these details will give the person with dementia information that they can consider and often discuss. We are then starting to put together stories.

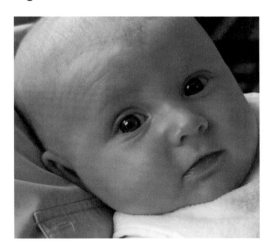 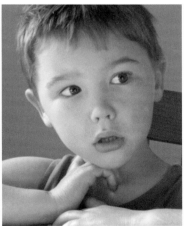

The image of a baby looking directly out at the viewer engages us in a way that the image of the thoughtful boy doesn't. Someone with dementia may still be successfully engaged by the photograph of the boy, but it would depend more on having some additional context that gave clues about what he was looking at or thinking about.

Narrative and making up stories

When an image contains a combination of elements, with people, objects or animals, and these elements are engaged in some sort of activity, then the person with dementia can be encouraged to take part in a form of story telling. This may be related in some way to their own emotions or memories or may be completely whimsical and creative.

Even when a person has no speech, a carer can talk about what they imagine might be happening in the picture.

This 'story telling' is a creative act and is truly living in the moment. It may have little to do with reminiscence and is about enjoying the moment with a picture that captures the imagination.

The painting opposite 'Going into the World' by Evert-Jan Boks is the type of image that has great storytelling potential. Where is the lady going? What sort of a person is she? Is she wealthy? Is she someone who has to work for a living? Is she married? Who is the rather creepy looking man around the corner and what is he thinking? Where is the station? Are there clues on the wall behind her? And what is the scrap of paper lying on the floor?

This image has many attributes that make it suitable for people with dementia. The clarity of the image and the clear outline of the woman; the strong contrasts between her dark jacket and the lighter wall behind her; the way she is looking straight out at the viewer; the lack of too much depth or three-dimensional complexity; a fairly simple background setting with another figure looking towards the viewer; enough in the image to give clues as to what is happening (the travel chest and the timetables) without too much complexity; the relevance of waiting for a train - something that many people will have done. There is the opportunity to imagine how the woman is feeling and this can sometimes tap into the emotions of the viewer with dementia. If they are feeling lonely and afraid, they may well imagine that the woman in the painting is also feeling that way, and this can give carers an opportunity to offer reassurance and comfort.

'Going into the World' by Evert-Jan Boks (1839-1914) Getty Images

Texture in images

Often if the image is of a high quality and has great level of detail so that the texture of the surface can be seen clearly, the person with dementia will stroke the image whether it is a dog, a baby's face or some embroidery.

Sometimes carers feel that people with dementia would benefit from images that include 'touchy feely' textures. They have often seen the books for babies that are produced with a range of images incorporating textures and see this type of resource as potentially being helpful. However, if we consider why babies have such books we can understand why people with dementia don't need them.

Babies are learning all about their world. They may have never stroked a furry creature or a shiny mirror. They are experiencing all these things for the first time and are starting to understand what different textures feel like. By the time they go to school at 4 years old they are usually confident about what the majority of textures feel like.

Someone with dementia learned what most things feel like to touch many years ago and it is very likely that they retain that knowledge. If something in an image leads them to stroke the paper it may well be that they are experiencing the texture in their mind.

Chapter 3
Using picture books to improve care

Few people would argue that meaningful occupation and communication for people with dementia is key to really good dementia care. But meaningful occupation and communication is not just the regular musical entertainment or a one-off flower arranging session. It requires small meaningful activities that go on throughout the day (or night) seven days a week. Five minutes spent having a quiet chat, getting someone to help lay a table or do some dusting, wandering in the garden, sorting though a box of postage stamps; these are the types of activities that should be a normal part of every day.

For people with more advanced dementia the importance of providing small regular interventions is greater than for those with early stage dementia.

When people have lost the ability to self motivate, to get up and walk around and find some stimulation, they can be left in a chair, ignored because they are dozing and are no trouble, and it's difficult for staff to engage them.

To be able to provide small moments of contact throughout the day for people with advanced dementia, staff and relatives need simple and affordable resources. They don't need expensive touch screen computer technology or reminiscence rooms. People with dementia, whoever they are, just need the sort of everyday things that they might once have had at home, and that retain some relevance to them now in their current stage of dementia.

Illustrated books with the right pictures and text, and presented in the right format are one of the things that have the potential to provide small meaningful moments of contact at any time of day or night and in any setting. If designed to be attractive to the carer as much as the person with dementia, they place both 'carer' and 'cared for' on the same level, with no one having more power than the other. The joy of a book of beautiful pictures can be truly a shared experience.

The use of text within books is also something that many people feel is not appropriate for those with later stage dementia because they believe that people can no longer read. But if text is presented in the right format, often people in the later stages can still read and enjoy the written word.

This opens up opportunities for rediscovering songs, poetry and traditional sayings that are often not forgotten, even in the later stages of dementia. Many people with advanced dementia, when seeing a few words from a familiar song or poem written down in a way that is easy to read, will sing or recite them from memory.

The right books can continue to offer many people with advanced dementia a real opportunity to engage with the world and with other people in a remarkable and meaningful way. This can have added benefits for those who care for people with dementia by allowing them to get to know those they are caring for better, and by making their job more rewarding and enjoyable.

Research shows that using the right illustrated books can reduce depression and isolation and can also promote meaningful communication with someone with dementia when little else works.

Tom Kitwood (2004) identifies several different types of interaction involved in good dementia care, each one enhancing 'personhood' in a different way. These types of positive interaction are recognition, negotiation, collaboration, play, timalation (interaction that needs little cognitive understanding), celebration, relaxation, validation, holding (in a psychological sense), facilitation, creation and giving.

Photo - Methodist Homes

Below we can see how something as simple as a 'Pictures to Share' book can help to create these twelve types of interaction.

Recognition

Someone who has dementia is being acknowledged as a person, known by name, affirmed in his or her own uniqueness.

A carer or visitor approaches the person with dementia holding three different picture books. Looking into their eyes, the carer addresses them by name and touches their hand.

Negotiation

People who have dementia are being consulted about their preferences, desires or needs, rather than being conformed to other's assumptions.

The carer or visitor asks the person if they would like to look at a book together, and if so, asks them to choose one.

Collaboration

Two or more people aligned on a shared task.

The carer or visitor and the resident sit close together turning the pages and looking at the book together.

Play

Whereas work is directed towards a goal, play in its purest form has no goal that lies outside the activity itself.

Looking at picture books is seen by both resident and the carer or visitor as a recreational activity.

Timalation

This term refers to forms of sensual interaction in which there is minimal need for intellectual understanding. The significance of this kind of interaction is that it can provide contact, reassurance and pleasure, whilst making very few demands. It is thus particularly valuable when cognitive impairment is severe.

Without the need to use intellectual understanding to fully interpret what they see in the picture books, the person with dementia recognizes things that still have meaning. They respond with words, a smile, or by touching the image.

Celebration

Any moment at which life is experienced as intrinsically joyful. Celebration is the form of interaction in which the division between caregiver and cared-for comes nearest to vanishing completely; all are taken up into a similar mood.

A certain picture prompts the person with dementia to touch the picture and smile. The carer or visitor also responds to the image in the same way and both agree how beautiful the picture is.

A Pictures to Share book being shared between a lady with dementia and a young relative

Relaxation

Many people with dementia, with their particularly strong social needs, are only able to relax when others are near them, or in actual bodily contact.

Sitting close to the person with dementia looking at the books, and slowly turning the pages, the carer or visitor is quietly and calmly engaging in a relaxed manner with the person with dementia.

Validation

Acknowledging the reality of a person's emotions and feelings, and giving a response on the feeling level.

The person with dementia may have strong views about a picture and the carer or relative has the opportunity to share their feelings and so validate their response.

Holding

To hold in a psychological sense, means to provide a safe psychological space, where hidden trauma and conflict can be brought out; areas of extreme vulnerability exposed.

The person with dementia appears to be sad when looking intently at an image. Perhaps it is connecting with their own feelings of sadness or isolation. The carer or visitor has the opportunity to acknowledge this response and talk about these feelings to the person with dementia whilst trying to make the person feel secure and loved.

Facilitation

The task of facilitation is to enable interaction to get started, to amplify it and to help the person gradually fill it out with meaning.

The use of specially designed picture books facilitates a variety of interactions. By using the books with the person with dementia, the carer or visitor can enable an interaction. By sharing the experience they can also fill it with meaning.

Creation

Here a person with dementia spontaneously offers something to the social setting from his or her stock of ability and social skill.

The use of poetry, songs or traditional sayings in Pictures to Share books can often mean that the person with dementia has more knowledge than a young carer or a carer from another culture. This can shift the power balance in unexpected ways and make the person with dementia feel they still have something valuable to offer.

Giving

The person with dementia expresses concern, affection or gratitude.

The person with dementia thanks the carer or relative for spending time with them. They feel relaxed and content. He or she expresses this with a warm smile.

Conclusion

The visual arts and music are part of our civilisation that give life joy and meaning for most of us. The power of music to reach even some of those who seem completely unreachable has been seen many times. We just need to select the right choice of music to be meaningful to the individual. The form of the music itself needs little or no intervention from us to make it accessible for those with later stage dementia.

For many people the visual arts or books may have had more personal significance, and may be more successful in engaging them when they have dementia.

But pictures and the written word are not that simple to use when we have dementia. The neurological processes through which we understand and process visual imagery and text are highly complex and dementia interferes significantly with those processes. But as we have seen in these pages, given the right knowledge and understanding, these problems can be overcome.

If we make the effort to use the right pictures and the right texts we can help people with even very late stage dementia overcome these problems and stay more much meaningfully connected to the people and the world around them.

Photo - Methodist Homes

Pictures to Share books

Proverbs & Sayings

A World of Work
in pictures

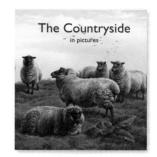

The Countryside
in pictures

Pets
in pictures

Travelling
in pictures

Family Life
in pictures

Beside the Seaside
in pictures

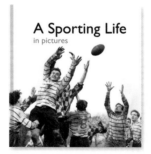

A Sporting Life
in pictures

A Funny Old World
in pictures

In the Garden
in pictures

Shopping
in pictures

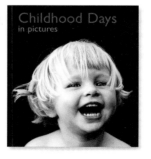

Childhood Days
in pictures

References & Useful Sources:

Brooker D. Person-Centred Dementia Care. Making services better. Jessica Kingsley 2007

Burns A., Winblad B., Severe Dementia. Wiley 2006

Kandel E.R. 'The Age of Insight' The quest to understand the unconscious in art, mind and brain.' Random House 2012

Kitwood T., Dementia Reconsidered. Open University 2004

Mackinlay E., Trevitt C. Finding meaning in the Experience of Dementia. The place of spiritual reminiscence work. Jessica Kingsley 2012

Miller D., The Comfort of Things. Polity Press 2008

Ramachandran V.S., The Tell-Tale Brain. Unlocking the mystery of human nature. Windmill Books 2012

Smith K., Moriarty S., Barbatsis G., Kenney K., Handbook of Visual Communication, Theory, Methods and Media. Routledge 2005

Smith P.T.M., Dementia Care, The Adaptive Response. Speechmark 2013

For more information on the
work of Pictures to Share including
research findings, please go to
www.picturestoshare.co.uk

Printed in England by
Langham Press
www.langhampress.co.uk